T0057085

Bob Chilcott
Carols 1

9 carols for mixed voices

MUSIC DEPARTMENT

OXFORD
UNIVERSITY PRESS

OXFORD
UNIVERSITY PRESS

Great Clarendon Street, Oxford OX2 6DP, England
198 Madison Avenue, New York, NY10016, USA

Oxford University Press is a department of the University of Oxford.
It furthers the University's aim of excellence in research, scholarship,
and education by publishing worldwide

Oxford is a registered trade mark of Oxford University Press
in the UK and in certain other countries

© Oxford University Press 2004

The Moral Rights of the author have been asserted
Database right Oxford University Press (maker)

This collection first published 2004

All rights reserved. No part of this publication may be reproduced,
stored in a retrieval system, or transmitted, in any form or by any means,
without the prior permission in writing of Oxford University Press,
or as expressly permitted by law. Enquiries concerning reproduction
outside the scope of the above should be sent to the Music Copyright Department,
Oxford University Press, at the address above

Permission to perform these works in this anthology in public
(except in the course of divine worship) should normally be obtained
from the Performing Right Society Ltd. (PRS), 29/33 Berners Street,
London W1T 3AB, or its affiliated Societies in each country throughout
the world, unless the owner or the occupier of the premises
being used holds a licence from the Society

Permission to make a recording must be obtained in advance
from the Mechanical Copyright Protection Society Ltd. (MCPS),
Elgar House, 41 Streatham High Road, London SW16 1ER,
or its affiliated Societies in each country throughout the world

13

ISBN 0-19-353233-6 978-0-19-353233-5

Music and text origination by Barnes Music Engraving Ltd., East Sussex
Printed in the United Kingdom on acid-free paper by
Halstan Printing Group, Amersham.

Contents

Christmas-tide	6
For Him all Stars have Shone	10
Lully, lulla, thou little tiny child	18
Mid-winter	26
Nova! nova!	33
Remember, O thou man	37
The Shepherd's Carol	45
The Time of Snow	53
Where Riches is Everlastingly	62

Preface

These nine pieces represent almost all of the mixed-voice carols I have written over the last ten years. The first to appear, *Mid-winter*, was originally written in 1994 as an upper-voice carol for the Toronto Children's Chorus, but is included here in a version for mixed voices. Most of the texts for these pieces will be well known and loved by choir singers, but I hope that one or two will be new, among them the folk-like text of *The Shepherd's Carol* which was suggested by the Dean of King's College, Cambridge. It was at the service where this was first sung that I heard a reading of the beautiful Elizabeth Jennings poem used here in *For Him all Stars have Shone*. Another woman poet, the American Janet Lewis, is represented in the gentle and human poem *Christmas-tide*, and the text of *The Time of Snow* is mine.

I would like to thank Robin Barry, who has encouraged so much of the work in this book.

Bob Chilcott
May 2004

for Joanne Hart

Christmas-tide

Janet Lewis (1899–1998)

BOB CHILCOTT (b. 1955)

Also available separately: BC15; ISBN 978-0-19-343218-5

Text reproduced by permission of Ohio University Press
This piece © Oxford University Press 1997 and 2004
This collection © Oxford University Press 2004

Printed in Great Britain

OXFORD UNIVERSITY PRESS MUSIC DEPARTMENT, GREAT CLARENDON STREET, OXFORD OX2 6DP
Photocopying this copyright material is ILLEGAL.

10
the Lord of ev - ery - thing?
in her womb should sleep and grow
oo
12
mp cresc.
Lul - lee, lul - lay, an an - gel stood with her who
mp cresc.
p
15
said,
unis.
mf cantabile
'That which doth stir like sum - mer in thy side shall
mp cresc.

17
cresc.
save the world from sin. Then sta - ble, hall and inn shall che - rish
cresc.
19
rit.
slower
a tempo
unis. p dolce
Lul - lee, lul-lay, and
unis.
Christ-mas-tide.'
p dolce
rit.
slower
a tempo
p dolce
22
so it was that Day. And did she love Him more be - cause an

24
p poco cresc.
an-gel came to pro-phe-sy His name? Ah no, not so, she
p poco cresc.
p poco cresc.
27
p
could not love Him more, but loved Him just the same.
p
p
30
p dolce
rit.
pp
slower
Lul-lee, lul-lee, lul-lee, lul lay.
p dolce
pp
rit.
slower
pp

Commissioned by the Cheyenne Chamber Singers for the Cheyenne Chamber Singers and the All-City Children's Chorus, conductor Jane Iverson

For Him all Stars have Shone

Elizabeth Jennings (1926–2001)

BOB CHILCOTT (b. 1955)

Also available separately: BC57; ISBN 978-0-19-343301-4. The upper-voice part to this arrangement is available as a separate leaflet: ISBN 978-0-19-343335-9. A version for 4-part upper voices and piano appears in *For Him all Stars: 15 carols for upper voices*: ISBN 978-0-19-335569-9

Text by Elizabeth Jennings; by permission of David Higham Associates.
© Oxford University Press 2002 and 2004. Photocopying this copyright material is ILLEGAL.

11
And care-ful shep - herds look u-pon the one un-sul - lied
14
TUTTI
mp espress.
div.
birth.
They kneel and stare while time seems gone and
mp espress.
17
unis.
rit.
a tempo
good-ness rules the earth.
mp più espress.

21
S.
A.
SOPRANO
ALTO
pp
He is so small the
T.
B.
TENOR
BASS
pp
poco cresc.
pp
24
stars bow down
The fierce winds ease their breath,
27
cresc.
And care-ful shep-herds look u-pon the one un-sul - lied
cresc.
cresc.

30
UPPER-VOICE CHOIR
mp espress.
They kneel and stare while time seems
mp espress.
S.
A.
birth. They kneel and stare while time seems gone and
T.
B.
mp espress.
mp espress.
33
rit.
a tempo
gone, gone, gone.
unis.
good-ness rules the earth.
unis.
rit.
a tempo
p dolce e sost.

37
SOPRANOS
p dolce
The blight on man is all un-done, And there will be no_
40
For though this_ child
mp cresc.
S.
A.
death, For though this child
will be nailed on a cross, he'll_
For though this_ child
T.
B.
mp cresc.
though this child
mp cresc.

43
f
mf dim.
S.
be so since he is the jewel of un - told worth,
A.
be so since he is the jewel of
T.
be so since he is the jewel of un - told
B.
be so since he is the
mp dim.
46
rit.
a tempo
UPPER-VOICE CHOIR
p legato espress.
For him all
un - told worth,
For him all
worth,
For him all stars have
pp
jewel of un - told worth,
For him all stars have
p

50
stars have shone,
For him all stars have shone,
p legato espress.
all stars have shone,
all stars have
stars have shone,
stars have shone, have
shone,
stars have shone,
shone,
stars have shone,
53
pp
For him all stars have shone,
for him all stars have
shone,
pp
all stars have shone,
pp
shone,
For him all stars have shone,
stars have
pp
For him all stars have shone,
stars have
pp
For him all stars have shone,
stars have
pp

56
rit.
a little slower
p
shone,
have
shone,
shone,
have
shone,
shone,
shone,
have
shone,
shone,
shone,
have
shone,
shone,
shone,
have
shone,
shone,
rit.
a little slower
59
rit.
shone.
S.
A.
shone.
T.
B.
rit.
p dolce
pp

for Michael Kibblewhite and Cantate Youth Choir

Lully, lulla, thou little tiny child

15th century

BOB CHILCOTT (b. 1955)

© Oxford University Press 2004. Photocopying this copyright material is ILLEGAL.

11
lit-tle ti - ny child, By by, lul - ly lul - lay.
By by, lul - ly lul - lay.
lit-tle ti - ny child, By by, lul - ly lul - lay.
17
S.
mp
cresc.
O sis - ters too, How may we do For to pre - serve this
A.
mp
cresc.
23
mf
mp
day This poor young - ling, For whom we do sing, By by, lul - ly lul -
mf
mp

30
S.
- lay? Lul - ly, lul - la, thou lit-tle ti - ny child, By by, lul -
A.
- lay? Lul - ly, lul - la, lul - la, By by, lul - ly
T.
Lul - ly, lul - la, thou lit-tle ti - ny child, By by, lul -
B.
Lul - ly, lul - la, By by,
Pno
p
37
- ly lul - lay, thou lit-tle ti - ny child, By by, lul -
lul - lay, lul - ly, lul - la, By by,
- ly lul - lay, thou lit-tle ti - ny child, By by, lul -
lul - lay, lul - la, By by, lul -

43
-ly lul - lay.
lul - ly lul - lay.
-ly lul - lay.
mf
He - rod, the king, In his ra -
-ly lul - lay.
mf
49
T.
B.
cresc.
f
- ging, Char - gèd he hath this day His men of
cresc.
f
54
mf
might, In his own sight, All young child - ren to
mf

59
S.1
Lul - ly, lul - la, By by, lul -
S.2
Lul - ly, lul - la, thou lit - tle ti - ny child, By by, lul -
A.
Lul - ly, lul - la, lul - la, By by, lul - ly
T.
slay. Lul - ly, lul - la, thou lit - tle ti - ny child, By by, lul -
B.
slay. Lul - ly, lul - la, By by,
Pno
p
66
- ly lul - lay, lul - ly, lul - la, By
- ly lul - lay, thou lit - tle ti - ny child, By by, lul -
lul - lay, lul - ly, lul - la, By by,
- ly lul - lay, thou lit - tle ti - ny child, By by, lul -
lul - lay, lul - la, By by, lul -

72
p
by lul - lay. That woe is me, Poor child for thee!
-ly lul - lay. That woe is me, Poor child for thee!
lul - ly lul - lay. That woe is me, Poor child for thee!
-ly lul - lay. That woe is me, Poor child for
-ly lul - lay. That woe is me, Poor child for
79
TUTTI
cresc.
mp
S.
And e - ver morn and day, For thy par - ting Nei-ther say nor sing
A.
And e - ver morn and day, For thy par - ting Nei-ther say nor sing
T.
thee! And e - ver morn and day, For thy par - ting Nei-ther say nor
B.
thee! And e - ver morn and day, For thy par - ting,

86
S.1
By by, lul - ly lul - lay!
S.2
By by, lul - ly lul - lay! Lul -
A.
By by, lul - ly lul - lay! Lul - ly,
T.
sing By by, lul - ly lul - lay! Lul -
B.
By by, lul - ly lul - lay!
p
pp
91
Lul - ly, lul - la, By by, lul - ly lul -
- ly, lul - la, thou lit - tle ti - ny child, By by, lul - ly lul -
lul - la, lul - la, By by, lul - ly lul - lay,
- ly, lul - la, thou lit - tle ti - ny child, By by, lul - ly lul -

97
S.1
-lay, lul - ly, lul - la, By
S.2
-lay, thou lit-tle ti - ny child, By by, lul -
A.
lul - ly, lul - la, By by,
T.
-lay, thou lit-tle ti - ny child, By by, lul -
pp
B.
lul - la, By by, lul -
102
rit.
by lul - lay.
-ly lul - lay.
lul - ly lul - lay, lul - ly lul - lay.
-ly lul - lay.
-ly lul - lay.
rit.

Mid-winter

Christina Rossetti (1830–94)

BOB CHILCOTT (b. 1955)

Also available separately: BC3; ISBN 978-0-19-343194-2 and in a version for upper voices and piano: BC1; ISBN 978-0-19-341523-2
2 different orchestral accompaniments are available for rental. Brass: 2tpt, hn, tbn, tba, hp, pno Orchestra: 2fl, 2ob, 2cl. 2bsn, 2hn, hp, str

© Oxford University Press 1995 and 2004. Photocopying this copyright material is ILLEGAL.

10
SOPRANO
mp espress.
ALTO
stone;
Snow had fal - len,
snow on
TENOR
BASS
mp espress.
mp espress.
13
mf
snow,
In the bleak mid - win - ter, long a -
mp
mp
snow, on snow,
bleak mid - win - ter, long a -
mf
mp
mf
mp
17
p
mp
- go,
long a - go.
Our
p
mp
p
dolce

21
cresc.
God, heav'n can - not hold him nor_ earth sus - tain:
cresc.
mp pesante
25
cresc.
Heav'n and earth shall flee a-way when he comes to reign:
cresc.
cresc.
29
f
place_ suf - ficed_____ The_
mf
In the bleak mid - win - ter a sta - ble - place, a place__ suf - ficed__
f
f espress.

33
Lord God Al - might - y Je - sus Christ.
mf
Lord God Al - might - y Je - sus Christ.
mf
mf
37
f con forza
An - gels and arch - an - gels may have ga - thered there,
f con forza
f
Ped.
sim.
40
Che - ru-bim and se - ra-phim thronged the

44
f espress.
air; But on - ly his mo - ther in her
f espress.
f espress.
47
S. & A. unis.
mf
mai - - den bliss Wor - shipped the be -
mf
T. & B. unis.
mf
50
mp
S.
A.
- lo - ved with a kiss.
T.
B.
mp
mp
mf espress.

53
poco rit.
mp
p dolce
57
a tempo
SOPRANO & ALTO unis. p dolce
What can I give him,
Ped. sost.
sim.
61
poor as I am? If I were a
64
shep - herd I would bring a lamb;

67
mp espress.
S.
A.
I would do my part;
If I were a wise man I would do, would do my
T.
B.
mp espress.
mp espress.
mf
70
Yet what I can I give him– Give my heart,
mp
part; what I can I give him– Give my heart,
mp
mp
p
74
p
give my heart,
my heart.
poco rit.
a bit slower
pp
p
pp
poco rit.
a bit slower
dolce
pp

for David Hill and The Bach Choir
in celebration of the 80th Birthday of Sir David Willcocks

Nova! nova!

15th century (slightly modernized)

BOB CHILCOTT (b. 1955)

[1] *Nova! nova! 'Ave' fit ex 'Eva'.* = News! news! *'Ave'* ('hail') *is made from 'Eva'* ('Eve').

First appeared in *Advent for Choirs* edited by Malcolm Archer and Stephen Cleobury (ISBN 978-0-19-353025-6). Also available separately: BC46; ISBN 978-0-19-343300-7

© Oxford University Press 2000 and 2004. Photocopying this copyright material is ILLEGAL.

[2] I-wys = indeed [3] wened = thought

55
f
-a - ve'_ fit ex 'E - va'.
unis.
mp
Then said the an - gel: 'Dread not you, You
59
T./B.
shall con-ceive in all ver - tue A Child whose name shall be Je - su'.
63
S.
A.
p
pp
unis.
Oh, oh No - va!_ no - va! 'A - ve'_ fit
T.
B.
unis.
No - va!_ no-va!
p
pp
68
'It
mp
ex 'E - va'._ No - va!_ no - va!_ 'A - ve'_ fit ex 'E - va'.
73
is not yet six months a - gone Since E - li - za-beth con - ceiv - ed_ John, As
S.
A.
mm mm mm mm mm
77
it was pro-phe - sied ere long.'_
unis.
mf
S.
A.
mm No - va!_ no-va! No-no-no-
T./B.
f
Oh, oh No - va!_

[4] *Ecce ancilla Domini* = Behold the handmaid of the Lord.

for Gillian Dibden and the Berkshire Youth Choir

Remember, O thou man

Thomas Ravenscroft? (*c.*1582–1635)

BOB CHILCOTT (b. 1955)

Also available separately BC89; ISBN 978-0-19-335635-1.
First appeared in *Christmas Spirituals for Choirs* compiled by Bob Chilcott and Ken Burton (ISBN 978-0-19-343541-4)

© Oxford University Press 2003 and 2004. Photocopying this copyright material is ILLEGAL.

5
p cresc.
Re - mem - ber, O thou man, thy time is spent:
p cresc.
p cresc.
7
mf
Re - mem - ber, O thou man, how thou art dead and gone,
mf
mf
9
mp
and I did what I can: there - fore re - pent!
mp
mp

11
S.
A.
p
oo
T.
p
oo
B.
mp espress.
Re - mem - ber God's good - ness,
mp espress.
13
cresc.
oo
cresc.
oo
O thou man, O thou man,
cresc.
Re - mem - ber God's good - ness,
cresc.

15
mf
(oo)
(oo)
f
(oo)
Re - mem - ber God's good - ness;
mf
and pro - mise made!
oo
mf
17
sent his Son, doubt - less,
p
(oo)
oo
O
p
how he sent his Son, doubt - less,
oo
O
mp
(oo)
our sins for to re - dress;
mp

19
be not a - fraid!
The an - gels all did sing,
be not a - fraid!
The an - gels all did sing,
be not a - fraid!
The an - gels all did sing,
21
S.
A.
O thou man,
O thou man,
The an - gels all did sing
T.
B.

23
ff
On heav'ns high hill! The an - gels all did sing
ff
ff
25
dim.
prai - ses to our heav'n - ly King,
dim.
dim.

mp
and peace to man li - ving with a good will.
mp
mp
p
28
pp
To Beth - lem did they go,
pp
30
O thou man, O thou man,
poco cresc.
To Beth - lem did they go
poco cresc.

32
the shep - herds three; To Beth - lem did they go To
34
see whe - ther it were so, whe - ther Christ was born or no to set man
36
S.
A.
free, to set man free.
T.
B.
Pno

for Stephen Cleobury and the Choir of King's College, Cambridge

The Shepherd's Carol

ve Sansom (1910-81)

BOB CHILCOTT (b. 1955)

Gentle and with flexibility (♩. = *c.*36)

p semplice

SOPRANO

We stood on the hills, La - dy, Our day's work done,

PIANO *for rehearsal only*

p

5

S.

Watch-ing the frost - ed mea-dows That win-ter had won.

.1

pp

Calm,

.2

pp

Calm, calm,

pp

Also available separately: BC44; ISBN 978-0-19-343296-3

Music: © Oxford University Press 2001 and 2004. Words: The Shepherd's Carol by Clive Sansom, reproduced by permission of David Higham Associates Ltd. Photocopying this copyright material is ILLEGAL.

9
S.1
pp
Calm,
calm,
S.2
pp
Calm,
calm,
calm,
A.1
calm,
calm,
calm,
A.2
calm,
calm,
T.
p
The even-ing was calm,
La - dy,
The air so

Si - lence more love - ly than mu - sic
calm, Si - lence more love - ly than mu - sic
Si - lence, si - - lence,
calm, Si - lence,
pp
still, Si - lence more love - ly than mu - sic
pp
Si - - lence,
pp
Si - - lence, si - -
pp

16
S.
A.
unis.
si - lence, si - lence, mm
T.
p
Fold-ed the hill mm
B.1
si - lence, si - lence, mm
B.2
- - lence, si - lence, mm mm
20
p unis.
There was a star, La - dy, Shone in the night,
There was a star, La - dy, Shone in the night,
There was a star, La - dy, Shone in the night,
B.
There a star shone

3
cresc.
mf
f
Larg - er than Ve - nus it was and bright, so bright. Oh, a
Lar - ger than Ve - nus it was and bright, so bright. Oh, a
Lar - ger than Ve - nus it was and bright, so bright. Oh, a
and bright, so bright. Oh, a
26
ff appass.
voice from the sky, La - dy, It seemed to us then

30
S.
Of God be - ing born in the world of men.
A.
Of God be - ing born La - dy,
T.
Tel - ling of God be - ing born La - dy,
B.1
God be - ing born La - dy
B.2
God be - ing born La - dy, La -
33
p semplice
And
La - dy, mm
La - dy, mm
La - dy, mm
- dy, mm mm

36
so we have come, La - dy, Our day's work done, Our
T.
Our
40
p
love, our hopes, our - selves we give to your son.
Love, our - selves La - dy,
pp
love, our hopes, our - selves La - dy,
Love, our - selves La - dy,
Love, our - selves La - dy, La -

43
rit.
pp
mm
La - dy,
mm
mm
La - dy,
mm
mm
La - dy,
mm
mm
- dy,
mm
mm
mm
rit.
pp

The Time of Snow

BOB CHILCOTT (b. 1955)

Also available separately: BC56; ISBN 978-0-19-343312-0, and in a version for upper voices and piano; BC21; ISBN 978-0-19-342632-0
An orchestral accompaniment is available for rental. Hp, 2perc [susp cymb / glock, and triangle], str

© Oxford University Press 2002 and 2004. Photocopying this copyright material is ILLEGAL.

8
Ma-ry and Jo - seph, for e - ver blessed.
TENOR They
cresc.
cresc.
12
S.
cresc.
They tra-vel wea - ri - ly as they go, the time of win - ter, the
A.
cresc.
They tra - vel wea-ry as they go, the time,
T.
tra - vel wea - ri - ly as they go, the time, the
B.
cresc.
They tra - vel as they go,

15
time of snow.
the time of snow.
time of snow.
the time of snow.
p
18
mp
A place for shel - ter they have in mind,
mp
A place for shel - ter they have in mind,
mp
A place for shel - ter they have in mind,
mp
A shel - ter they have in mind,
mp

21
A sim - ple sta - ble is all they
A sim - ple sta - ble is all they
A sim - ple sta - ble is all they
A sta - ble is all they
24
cresc.
find. The pro-mise of an an - gel is all they know, the
cresc.
find. An an - gel is all they know,
cresc.
find. The pro-mise of an an - gel is all they know,
cresc.
find. An an - gel is all they know,
cresc.

27
time of win - ter, the time of snow.
the time, the time of snow.
the time, the time of snow.
the time of snow.
p
30
S.
A.
mp cresc.
It may not have been win-ter then,
T.
B.
mp cresc.
mp sonore

33
cresc.
that cer-tain night in Beth-le - hem, but with the beau-ty of this birth came
cresc.
cresc.
36
earth,
f
the re - new - al of the earth, of the earth,
f
f
ff

39
mp
as a flower that grows
p
through the melt - ing
mp
p
43
snows.
p
46
p dolce
There in the si - lence lies Ma - ry's
p dolce
p dolce

49
son,
a source of won - der for
52
S.
ev - ery - one.
poco cresc.
With-in a sta - ble so
A.
ev - ery - one.
poco cresc.
A sta - ble so
T.
ev - ery - one.
poco cresc.
With - in a sta - ble
B.
ev - ery - one.
poco cresc.
A sta - ble so
poco cresc.

55
long a - go, the time of win - ter, the time, the
long a - go, the time, the time, the
so long a - go, the time, the time, the
long a - go, the time, the
58
p
poco rit.
time of snow.
time of snow.
time of snow.
time of snow.
mp sonore
pp

for Michael Kibblewhite and Cantate Youth Choir

Where Riches is Everlastingly

16th century (adapted B.C.) BOB CHILCOTT (b. 1955)

The percussion parts are available to purchase separately from the publisher; ISBN 978-0-19-355845-8

© Oxford University Press 2004. Photocopying this copyright material is ILLEGAL.

10
and Man, Lord and ser - vant in one per - son,
lall lall lall lall Lall lall lall lall lall lall lall lall lall
13
Born of the Bles - sed Vir - gin Ma - ry. I pray you be mer - ry and
Lall lall lall lall lall lall lall la
gs
h.
b.
16
S.
sing with me In wor-ship of Christ's na - ti - vi - ty. I
A.
sing with me In wor-ship of Christ's na - ti - vi - ty. I
T.
B.

19
pray you be mer - ry and sing with me In wor-ship of Christ's na - ti -
pray you be mer - ry and sing with me In wor-ship of Christ's na - ti -
na - ti -
22
- vi - ty.
mf
- vi-ty. Lall lall lall lall lall lall lall lall lall Lall lall lall lall lall
- vi - ty.
mf

26
A.
lall lall lall lall Lall lall lall lall lall lall lall lall lall
unis. mf
T.
B.
He that was rich with - out a need Ap -
gs
29
Lall lall lall lall lall lall lall lall lall Lall lall lall lall lall
- peared in this world in right poor weed To make us that were poor
32
S.
SOPRANOS
f
I
A.
f
lall lall lall lall lall lall lall lall lall lall lall la I
T.
B.
f
in - deed, Rich with-out a - ny need tru - ly. I
gs
h.
f

35
S.
A.
pray you be mer - ry and sing with_ me In wor-ship of Christ's na - ti -
T.
B.
Cgs
f
Sh.
Cb.
f
38
S.
- vi - ty. I pray you be mer - ry and sing with_ me In
A.
- vi - ty. I pray you be mer - ry and sing with me In
T.
B.

41
mp
wor-ship of Christ's na - ti - vi - ty. A
mp
wor-ship of Christ's na - ti - vi-ty. Lall lall lall_ lall lall___ lall lall lall lall
unis. mp
wor-ship of Christ's na - ti - vi - ty. A
mp
45
sta - ble was his Cham - ber, a crib___ was his bed,___ He
Lall lall lall_ lall lall___ lall lall lall lall Lall lall lall_ lall lall___ lall lall lall lall
sta - ble was his Cham - ber, a crib___ was his bed,___ He

49
had not a pil - low un - der his head;
Lall lall lall lall lall lall lall lall lall Lall lall lall lall lall lall lall lall lall
had not a pil - low un - der his head;
Cgs
mp
Sh.
53
mp
S.1
Lall lall lall lall lall lall lall lall lall Lall lall lall lall lall lall lall lall lall
mf
S.2
With mai-den's milk that babe was fed, In
mp
A.
Lall lall lall lall lall lall lall lall lall Lall lall lall lall lall lall lall lall lall
mf
T.
B.
With mai-den's milk that babe was fed, In
mf
mf

57
sub. p
Lall lall lall lall lall lall lall lall lall Lall lall lall lall lall lall lall la I
sub. p
poor clothes was wrapped the Lord Al-migh - ty. I
sub. p
Lall lall lall lall lall lall lall lall lall Lall lall lall lall lall lall lall la I
poor clothes was wrapped the Lord Al-migh - ty.
61
f
pray you be mer - ry and sing with me In wor-ship of Christ's na - ti - vi - ty. I
f
pray you be mer - ry and sing with me In wor-ship of Christ's na - ti - vi - ty. I
f
I
mf
f

65
pray you be mer - ry and sing with me In wor-ship of Christ's na - ti -
pray you be mer - ry and sing with me In wor-ship of Christ's na - ti -
pray you be mer - ry and sing with me In wor-ship of Christ's na - ti -
Cgs
f
Sh.
Cb.
f
68
- vi - ty.
- vi - ty.
f
unis.
- vi-ty. Lall lall lall lall lall lall lall lall lall Lall lall lall lall lall

72
f
A no - ble les - son here is taught, To set all world-ly ri -
lall lall lall lall Lall lall lall lall lall lall lall lall lall Lall lall lall lall lall
76
-ches at naught, But pray that we may be thi - ther brought Where ri-ches is e - ver - last-
lall lall lall lall Lall lall lall lall lall lall lall lall lall Lall lall lall lall lall
80
f
- ing - ly. I pray you be mer - ry and sing with me In
lall lall la
f

83
S.
ff
wor-ship of Christ's na - ti - vi - ty. I pray you be mer-ry and sing with me In
A.
ff
wor-ship of Christ's na - ti - vi - ty. I pray you be mer-ry and sing with me In
T.
B.
ff
ff
ff
ff
87
wor-ship of Christ's na - ti - vi - ty.
wor-ship of Christ's na - ti - vi - ty.